FINDING THE WORDS TO
PRAY FOR YOUR CHILDREN

Motherhood Moments

DESI SOITARIDIS

Ark House Press
arkhousepress.com

© 2023 Desi Soitaridis

All rights reserved. Apart from any fair dealing for the purpose of study, research, criticism, or review, as permitted under the Copyright Act, no part may be reproduced by any process without written permission.

Scripture quotations marked NIV® are taken from the New International Version®, © 1973, 1978, 1984, 2011 by Biblica, Inc.® Used with permission. All rights reserved worldwide.
Scripture quotations marked THE MESSAGE are taken from The Message Bible. © by Eugene H. Peterson 1993, 2002, 2005, 2018. Used by permission of NavPress. All rights reserved. Represented by Tyndale House Publishers.
Scripture quotations marked AMP are taken from the Amplified Bible, © 2015 by The Lockman Foundation. Used by permission.
Scripture quotations marked ESV® are taken from the The Holy Bible, English Standard Version®, copyright © 2001 by Crossway, a publishing ministry of Good News Publishers. Used by permission. All rights reserved.

Some names and identifying details have been changed to protect the privacy of individuals.

Cataloguing in Publication Data:
Title: Motherhood Moments
ISBN: 9780645802566 (pbk)
Subjects: REL012130 [RELIGION / Christian Living / Women's Interests]; REL012120 [RELIGION / Christian Living / Spiritual Growth]; FAM034000 [FAMILY & RELATIONSHIPS / Parenting / General].
Other Authors/Contributors: Soitaridis, Desi
Design by initiateagency.com

DEDICATION

To my greatest gifts – my children.

You are eternally loved, deeply known, and always prayed for.

BEFORE YOU BEGIN

While my husband and I were struggling to conceive, we would hear many stories of parenthood. Some stories encouraged my dreamy ideal of motherhood, others made me consider if the fight was really worth it.

Then finally I fell pregnant and more well-meaning advice was given, "Enjoy your sleep while you can! Expect to be exhausted a lot of the time!" *Sleep, right, check, must do that.* "If you want to formula feed, don't feel bad, so many mothers end up formula feeding." *Remember to pack the formula in the hospital bag. Check.* "Have you thought about a sleep routine? I didn't bother, they are too restricting." *Baby cries, I feed. Got it. Check.* "Make sure your baby takes the dummy, so they don't suck their thumb. It's easier to remove a dummy than a thumb!" *Of course, a dummy! Why didn't I think of that? Pack that in the hospital bag. Check.* "Sleep when baby sleeps, don't worry about the housework." *Ok, rest is important. Check.* "Have you thought about when you're going back to work? It would be a shame to stop teaching after you have studied so hard." *Oh good, I already have a plan for that. Check.*

Finally, my little girl arrived. She came into the world full of excitement and curiosity, captivating her new Mummy and

Daddy. Then, it dawned on me, how am I supposed to do all the things people had recommended and still be a wife, a daughter, a sister, a friend, a teacher?

As any new mother does, I became a social media addict. Instagram posts and Google searches flooded my phone with handy tips to get your newborn to sleep, easy dinner menus, how to wean off night feedings, latest arrivals of baby clothing, must have items in a nursery and of course, beautiful glowing mothers, hair done, fresh-faced out for walks with their newborn babes. All the while, I was sitting on the couch in my track pants, half asleep and unsure if I brushed my teeth that morning.

I am sure that many new mothers face the same predicament, and if you are anything like me, I wanted to prove to myself, to my husband and to my family, that I could do it all without the help of anyone else around me.

So, I decided to read books. Not just any books, but Christian mothering books. There, as I flipped through pages and pages of encouragement, I realised that I wasn't called to be a mother who was concerned about the latest clothing arrivals and the routines of feeding and sleeping. I wasn't just a wife who cooked and cleaned for her husband and waited around all day for him to come home from work so I can ask him questions about his day. I wasn't just a daughter and a sister who called every so often, gave advice, sent pictures of their new niece and granddaughter. I wasn't just an English teacher, passionately desiring to speak life and truth into the students I taught. I was, and am, more importantly a child of God.

The weight of this realisation changed my perspective. Did I even really consider what it meant to be a Christian mother?

Did that mean I needed to pray more frequently? Read the Bible with my daughter? Help her memorise as many Bible verses as possible before the age of five? Was I spending enough time with God to even grow in my own spiritual walk?

Without adding more pressure, Sally Clarkson reminds her readers in *The Mission of Motherhood,* that the calling to be a mother has been placed on a woman's heart from the beginning of time, in Eden. It is the most fulfilling and rewarding role any woman can gratify because it reflects God's heart for His own children. Perhaps like so many other mothers, I knew that my primary responsibility to my daughter and any other child God would bless our family with, was to show them Christ, but I didn't know where to start.

On those mornings when I wished I was still asleep, the afternoons sitting on the play mat watching her play with her wooden toys, on the walks around the neighborhood and the evenings when I was depleted of energy; I felt too overwhelmed and exhausted to come to God and petition Him with my thoughts and prayers. I did my best to play children's Christian songs, pray with my daughter, tell her stories about God, but praying for her and for my family was put in the too-hard basket.

As I shared some of the books I was reading on my social media account, a mother messaged me in amazement that I had time to read. Once again, I was advised to enjoy my free time, because as children get older the demands become greater. This made me think, do all mothers shove God into their free time? Does God always just get second best as soon as we give birth? Is that enough for God and for us?

Psalm 24:1 tells us that, "The earth is the Lord's, and all it contains. The world, and those who dwell in it." God is present in everything. He is with us through it all. I imagine Him sitting with me on the couch as I type these words. He tells us, weary and burdened mothers, to come to Him so that He will give us rest (Matthew 11:28-30). We can freely speak to Him, anytime and anywhere. We can grab a coffee while the kids are napping and chat away, marvel at the flowers he created in our garden or thank Him for our meals. But some days, coming to Him means laying down one word from our fuzzy and over-filled minds. So, these were my thoughts as I sat down to begin writing this devotional of sorts.

This book contains twenty words we can bring to God and lay at His feet. It is not intended to be read in one sitting, like a novel. The words that I have used as a focus are ones that I found myself praying to God when I couldn't put sentences together. There are probably more in your own heart, for your own family and needs. The word itself can be something that sits and stirs within you over the week before you decide to move onto the next. There is no obligation, no command, nobody holding you to account. They are merely prompts, little reminders, to speak to God throughout the day, to seek and find Him with the word on your heart and mind, to pray these words over your children, your husband, your family, your friends and for yourself. Perhaps while you do the dishes, prepare dinner, feed your children, drive around the car park, or wait in line at the supermarket.

Let me tell you, a book about prayer is definitely not something I ever considered writing about. I have found myself constantly asking "Are you sure about this God?" But I hope to provide some hope to the mother who feels desperate, lost and not quite herself anymore. It's ok, God hears us even in our uttering. Please note that I am also no way equipped to share parenting advice and this is not my intention. What I want and feel called to share is my heart, my experiences and what I have learnt so far in my very short journey as a mother. I know that I, like so many mothers, have so much more to learn as my children grow and my family, Lord willing, expands. But with the endless voices that bombard our minds, I pray that you let these words help you speak truth and encouragement deep into your heart and your mind.

1

JOY

*I have told you these things so that
My joy and delight may be in you,
and that your joy may be made full
and complete and overflowing*
– John 15:11.

During the years of infertility, I was always frustrated at the constant disappointments and heartache. My husband knew God would give us children. But I doubted. I struggled so much to have joy in my life during that season. Waiting was tough, and there always seemed to be another thing to wait for.

When our daughter was nine months old, I suffered a horrible miscarriage at ten weeks pregnant. The physical, emotional, and spiritual pain left me depleted. On the outside, perhaps nobody could tell what was going on inside. My heart was aching for answers. When I thought I was done with heartbreak around pregnancy, this caught me by surprise.

I interpreted God's inaction towards my suffering as unloving, unkind, and uncaring. Because of that, I was robbed of joy. But what I learnt walking down the path of pain and confusion is that He does care, ever so deeply. Our joy is not based on a life without suffering, but it is despite suffering, in knowing that God is in control, His ways are good, and His ways are perfect. When we surrendered our lives to Christ we said, "God it doesn't matter if I have suffering in my life, if I face days of darkness, days that are unbearable, because I know that you are with me, I know that you walk the path alongside me, it is You who will sustain me."

Let's not confuse joy with happiness. While, of course, I want my children to be happy, that is not the end goal. Happiness is fleeting, happiness depends on emotions and circumstances. But *joy*, joy that fills the soul, that warms the heart, that coexists with grief and pain yet still holds on to hope and is flooded with peace - that is real joy. Joy is a byproduct of knowing Jesus. It is where nothing external, no emotion, no circumstance can change it. I know my children will experience hardships, I cannot stop that, yet I pray for those moments, that in the depth of sorrow they know God is real by the inexplicable joy inside them. This is God's joy.

What is robbing you of joy right now? Is it the inaction of God towards your suffering? Is it the endless routine and monotony?

We cannot find true joy on our own. Trust me, I have tried desperately. The earthly joy we constantly seek never satisfies, our heart yearns for more, something deeper. John 15:10-11 says, "Joy can be made full" only through Jesus who brings restoration to us. Likewise, Ezra encouraged the remaining Israelites to turn to God for restoration and he will provide the joy that will become their strength (Nehemiah 8:10).

It's hard to believe that Romans 8:18 tells us that God "ordains our deep disappointments and profound suffering for the sake of far greater joy" (Jon Bloom). Why would He do that to us? I am no theologian, but what I do know is that I have never grown, changed, repented, or drawn closer to God during the days I feel like I have everything under control. I have joy in the days of heartache, disappointments, and sadness because I have no control over those days. In the moments of suffering, I am being equipped to enjoy the moments of goodness, the greater joy in the better days, and more importantly, the great joy I will experience with my heavenly Father in heaven.

Here are some ways you can pray for joy:

- That no matter the circumstances, your heart will continually trust in God's goodness.
- For you to be reminded to be joyful and to see joy in everyday life.
- For your children to never lose their innocent joy as they grow into adulthood.
- That your children are strengthened in their days of darkness by God's spirit.
- That your marriage is strengthened by the hard days and enjoyed in the good days.
- For your friends and family, that they come to find the joy of the Lord.

2
PEACE

Peace, I leave with you; my peace I give you. I do not give to you as the world gives
– JOHN 14:27.

I recently heard the saying, "Oh honey, stop buzzing and just bee." While the state of the world during the last couple of years has forced everyone and everything to stop (thanks to COVID-19), it made me think that even in lockdown I am always trying to find things to keep me occupied. I'm too busy attending to the buzzing noise of my phone, checking emails and updates and attempting to stay connected with my family and the outside world. Yet the easiest way for me to disconnect with God is to have no time for Him.

Every morning, before we start the day, I play worship songs and Christian songs for my children through our Google Home. Throughout the week, we have our morning routine, I unload the dishwasher and get our breakfast ready, and the kids play with their toys and explore the house. Our music creates a soothing atmosphere as it plays along in the background. Now, my son is at the age where he can reach to open the kitchen cupboard doors, so he usually plays in the kitchen, opening up all the doors and looking back at me saying, "Don't touch," like I have instructed him several times before. The weekends though are a little different. Our mornings are slower, but a little crazy. We have eggs sizzling, kettle boiling, the coffee machine heating up, toast cooking, a three-year-old singing and a baby crying while he waits in his highchair for his breakfast. During those mornings, I find it extremely hard to hear the music playing over all the noise. I try to catch glimpses of the words, but of course, because everything is on at once, my husband has turned down the volume and it's impossible to hear. Until of course, the noises stop when we're all sitting at the table.

It is possible that you have heard many times through sermons, youth camps or just general Christian discussion, that it can be hard to hear the voice of God when the noises of the world are bombarding our minds. This is how I feel over the weekend - I struggle to hear God, and to focus on Him. But the reality is, for most of us, the noise, chaos, and busyness, is not just in the morning, it's throughout our whole day. While we're taking kids to school, folding clothes, making beds, driving to gymnastics, going grocery shopping, and everything in between, life seems so rushed and busy. When we finally sit, and "be still" (Psalm 46:10), we find that our exhaustion becomes too busy for God too.

In Audrey Barrick's article *Survey: Christians Worldwide Too Busy for God* she wrote: "In data collected from over 20,000 Christians with ages ranging from 15 to 88 across 139 countries, The Obstacles to Growth Survey found that on average, more than 4 in 10 Christians around the world say they 'often' or 'always' rush from task to task… The busy life was found to be a distraction from God among Christians around the globe… About 6 in 10 Christians say that it's 'often' or 'always' true that 'the busyness of life gets in the way of developing my relationship with God." These are staggering statistics. When people were supposed to slow down and enjoy life, thanks to the industrial revolution, we seem to have made up for all the spare time by adding more things to do, and more things to think about. It is making us too busy for the most important thing in our life – God.

I'm sure you've heard the saying that if you're too busy for God then you're too busy. You may want to read that again. As mothers, we can be so overwhelmed by so much, our newborn babies, the demands of motherhood, how you'll be able to get dinner ready in time while also holding your teething baby around the house, worried that you'll have visitors, and you can't even remember the last time you took out the vacuum. I find that it's these things that keep my mind just as busy, too busy to turn to God.

I can hear you asking, what does busyness have to do with peace? Well, I am the first to admit that I surely do not have peace when I am preoccupied. There are seasons where busyness cannot be helped, but there can be peace in the busy. I assure you that God too is in the busy and He is the one who brings peace in that time.

The verse in John 14:27 reminds us that peace is not something we randomly stumble across, and it's not set aside time throughout the day. Peace is given to us; it is bestowed graciously as a gift. I think of the word bestowed as a present, wrapped up with beautiful wrapping, something that would excite my spirit and my heart as I open it. I laugh at that thought; I wonder how many mothers would love the present of peace!

This is exactly what God says He is giving us in this verse. However, it mentions here that the peace that will be given is not the peace we expect, not as the world, or our well-meaning friends would offer it. It is His peace. In the chaos of our lives, the busyness in our minds, God's peace satisfies us. It gives us a spirit of joy, an eye to see the needs of our children without getting frustrated, an ear to listen intently at our spouses, a heart that yearns to know God deeply and intimately.

But first we must accept His peace. We must accept the gift He is offering. Without accepting it, we are unable to feel it, see it and embrace it when we need it most.

I love the description of peace shared in L. S. P.'s poem:

> "My peace I give in times of deepest grief…
> when prayer seems lost, unheard…
> when you are left alone…
> in times of utter loss…
> when enemies will blame…
> in agony and sweet…
> when nearest friend betrays…
> [and] when there's but death for thee."

What are you relying on to give you peace? Have you truly accepted God's gift given to you? What is keeping your mind and your body preoccupied? Are you taking the opportunity to be present with your family, friends, and God when they're given to you?

Here are some ways you can pray for peace:

- Pray that God keeps your eyes open to see Him throughout your day.
- Pray for your children to feel and come to understand His peace.
- Pray for peace to surround your home.
- Ask God that even in the craziness of life, your spirit is constantly surrounded by God's gift of peace.

3
COMPASSION

*Finally, all of you, be like-minded,
be sympathetic, love one another,
be compassionate and humble*
– 1 Peter 3:8.

In my mind gentleness and kindness are mixed into one category – compassion. While they each have different meanings and purposes, for the discussion of prayer, I will blend them together.

When we ask God to help our children to be compassionate, we're asking for Him to help our children see the needs of others, to love people, to do good in this world, to be sincere, and to have a heart like Jesus. We want them to approach people with empathy, understanding, care, humility and in a fair and wise way.

Consider this: who are the people we are most drawn to in this world? For me, probably the ones who listen, the ones who show they care, the ones who speak with love, sincerity, and life. Isn't that who we want our children to be?

When I was completing my master's degree, I remember doing a character portfolio on Jesus as the ultimate example of a leader. What I discovered is that we see Jesus being interested in people, asking questions, He spent time with His Father.

He met people where they were at, He trained and equipped people, He knew they would fall short, but he let them try so that they would learn to grow. He showed grace in truth, He was humble and submissive, relational, and full of compassion throughout it all. When we share the character of Jesus and look deeply at His encounters with people in the New Testament, we can see a great example of what compassion looks like in real life. Jesus says in Matthew 11:29 that we should "learn" from Him, for He is "gentle and humble in heart." He doesn't say to just talk about Him or reflect on Him, but instead to copy and imitate Him, in all facets of life.

Real compassion is hard to find in our culture. Many times, this masks a person's personal gain and sometimes even prejudice. 1 Peter 3:8 specifically encourages Christians to be "likeminded... sympathetic... [loving]... compassionate and humble." But what stops us from being that way to all people? How much will our children share the love of Jesus if they have these virtues throughout all their lives?

As mothers, we might find it easier to show compassion to the lady serving us at the supermarket than it is to show it to our back chatting teenager or whining toddler. It takes a lot of effort to crucify our fleshly nature and remember that we are examples of Jesus to our families and little ones. When we are in the moment of frustration, our compassion seems to disappear.

Learning how to be an example of Jesus takes work. It doesn't happen overnight. As new Christians, we may start questioning why we aren't seeing the fruits of God in us immediately. But that's the thing with fruit - they begin as seeds, then grow into trees that bear fruit. We can't expect to be just like Jesus overnight, nor does He expect that of us. As we continue to be intimately connected with Him, we naturally begin to transform into an image bearer of His. Our experiences and daily encounters help to refine our character, and they help us grow in compassion.

Let's remember that this is the same for our children. They are only new to this world. They are learning right from wrong and all things in between. Showing compassion will be hard for them at a young age. We see it in the way we coax them to share their toys and speak kindly to their siblings. Slowly, slowly, we are to train their hearts to see the preciousness of others because we are all made in the image of God.

Here are some ways you can pray for compassion:

- Ask God to help you show compassion towards your family, even in times of frustration.
- Pray for wisdom and parenting the heart of your child.
- Pray for God to help you raise compassionate and loving children - those who see the best in people and treat others with respect.
- Ask God to help you grow into an intimate relationship with Him so that you may be a reflection of His character onto others, and likewise for your children.

*Now faith is the assurance of
things hoped for, the conviction
of things not seen*
– Hebrews 11:1.

When you look around you, sometimes all you can see is suffering. This year alone has been one filled with sorrow. For one, we have people dying from natural causes, or some who are suffering illnesses, then with the added COVID-19 cases. There are financial pressures, people losing their jobs, poor mental health, and just day-to-day struggles.

Our hearts yearn to be released from suffering. If you don't believe me, think about how many times you have gone to the doctor when you've been sick, or researched how to get out of a particular predicament. So, who or what can provide the ultimate deliverance?

You have probably heard the famous prayer by Augustine, where he begins by saying, "You have made us for yourself, and our heart is restless until it rests in you." I have this image in my mind of my daughter waiting at a café for her hot chips and babyccino. The excitement, shown in the movement of her hands and body as she attempts to wait ever so patiently for her food. She is restless, she cannot help it, despite the number of times we tell her to sit still. What Augustine is saying here is that a person desires rest and peace, but our lives and souls will continually be restless (fidgety and impatient, a bit like my daughter at a café) until it has found Jesus. Nothing else will satisfy this longing.

While our souls are restless, our hearts become troubled. We start to question God, His goodness and ultimately why we even trust Him. Faithfulness means trusting wholeheartedly, with no doubt or reservation. As I write this, I ask myself whether I trust God, whether I am faithful to Him. Just today, I received some medical news that I had no control over. Am I trusting that God is present in my suffering? Am I trusting that He knows better and is providing a way?

As for our children, we pray that they hold on to faith, that they find rest for their hearts in troubled times. We pray for our own faith in knowing they are taken care of when we see them walk into the kindergarten gates for the first time or go to their first sleepover. God tells us in John 14:1-4, don't be troubled by this world, the suffering, and the disappointments; trust *Me*, give your kids to *Me*, give your life to *Me*, put your faith in *Me*. As people, we are very good at keeping ourselves busy with worry and being practical in strategy, that we forget that all God asks for is for our faith, our trust, in Him.

During infertility, faith is what pulled me through. Faith has nothing to do with how worthy or good I am. It is about trusting in a God who holds it all in His hands; the good, the bad, the in-between. I had to hold onto the faith that no matter the outcome, God's ways are always bigger and better, even when I am crushed in spirit.

The verse at the beginning of this chapter, Hebrews 11: 1, has been used many times to define faith, but for this context, it reinforces my point; faith assures us that there is a God, a ruler over this world and everything in it. By believing that statement, trusting it, having *faith* in it and in God, we know that He has better things ahead of us, things that are not seen now or may not even be seen for a very long time. There will be so many moments in our lives, and in those of our children where we forget God's rightful place in this world; we forget who He is and what He has done. But we must remember that we have the assurance of a true and living God, who works behind the scenes, in moments we sometimes cannot see, for our good because He loves us. In the suffering, in the confusion, in the times when our schedules and day-to-day activities aren't going the way we plan, we surrender it to the Lord. We pray for peace and remind our hearts and minds that God is in control. We ask God to go before us in our days and to give us the trust we need to rely on Him.

Where do we put our faith? Who do we trust when things don't go the way we plan? I'll be the first to admit that I don't always turn to Jesus. So, what does faith look like for our families?

Here are some ways to pray for faith:

- Ask God to give you the faith to let go of the hurt, disappointment maybe even fear in your heart, and to find rest in Him.
- Pray that God leads you to be a good example to your family on leaving your troubles at the feet of Jesus.

- Pray that your children grow in faith so that they are strong when days of trouble come.

5
PURPOSE

The Lord will fulfil his purpose for me
– Psalm *138*:8.

I recently received an email from the high school I attended asking for past students to write about where they are now and what they're doing in their careers. I had the email sitting in my inbox for a while before I decided to delete it without replying. What did I have to say about my life after school? I didn't do anything extra significant or choose an excelling career. I didn't travel overseas and volunteer weeks or months of my time to teach English in an orphanage nor did I pursue my very limited sporting skills and travel around the world, with the hope to make it to the Olympics one day. Instead, I went to university, married my darling husband, and became a secondary school teacher in a Christian school. Now, I'm currently on maternity leave and just living mum-life at home. Sometimes I even wonder whether my parents regret sacrificing so much for me to go to a grammar school only to become a teacher. What words of wisdom could I impart to my past school community about normal, everyday motherhood?

As I consider these thoughts, I ask myself, do I really believe that I have no purpose in this world? Do I really believe that God sent His Son to die in my place because I am nothing and have no value to Him at all? Of course, I don't. God has a plan and a purpose for my life and for every life on this earth. What, in my mind, might look mundane, tiresome, and unfulfilling, is actually given to me as a blessing to praise and honor my Lord. Do I then live my life as though I am living my purposed life? Well sometimes I don't think I do. Sometimes, in the middle of naptime, cleaning the floors for the one-hundredth time, and packing away stuffed toys, I struggle to see my purpose. But it is there.

Perhaps the place you are in now seems too hard for you to manage. Perhaps you are bored, weary, longing for more. Perhaps you have a child who is going wayward, a child who challenges you beyond belief or one that *does not* stop crying (I have one of those)! Perhaps you have a husband who doesn't seem to understand your heart or mind. Even more challenging, and perhaps the most gut-wrenching, what if your child decides to turn away from God? For you, dear friend, the mother carrying this burden, I know one thing, there is nobody beyond God's reach - no wayward child, no fault in training or parenting, especially with a praying mother. Perhaps your days are filled with silent suffering, and it just seems like nobody will understand. Today, I want to remind you that God does. He knows you and made you, and loves you. He has given you enough to face this day. You don't need to do it alone. He has purposed you for this very moment, for your very family, for your very child. There is no better mother or wife or role model for your family than you. Do you believe that?

Charles Spurgeon once said that we are "as much serving God in looking after [our] own children, and training them up in God's fear, and minding the house, and making [our] household a church for God, as you would be if you had been called to lead an army to battle for the Lord of Hosts." Perhaps in our humble eyes, the everyday things don't matter, but to God they do. Mothers, we will not be in history books. There will be no earthly record on how many times we read the Bible to our children, how many times we prayed, how many meals we dropped off to our neighbours in need, how many times we opened our homes to shelter people. But we know that these moments are important to God, for it is these everyday moments that God's gospel is shown and shared.

In this world, where we celebrate a person's position over perseverance, we forget that our children are on a journey, and so are we. This life is not about reaching a pivotal moment, obtaining that job title, being debt free or owning that double story home. Our life is about those moments that get us there, the moments where we haven't felt worthy, or we've been disappointed, where we've experienced our greatest joys and have come away with stories to tell. That is where God is, in the everyday.

We need to do everyday things to show our children that God is meeting us where we are. This is how we "train up" our children. They see us using the skills and abilities that He has provided us to perform our everyday tasks. As Louisa May Alcott wrote, "The humblest tasks get beautified when loving hands do them." Our day-to-day may look boring, meaningless and uninspiring, but they are beautiful moments that share our love towards our family, towards others and towards God. Let our children see this in us. Let us be visionaries for our children, mothers who get into the hearts of our kids, to inspire them to find who they are in Jesus, to understand their purpose, to show kindness to all people and to seek Jesus with all their hearts.

As we look at the verse from Psalm 138:8, the word "fulfill" indicates that something is completed. God will complete what He has purposed for you, and He won't leave you or forsake you until it is achieved, and you are in His glory.

While you may be struggling with your purpose, your children are growing up to find out theirs. As all mothers do, I sometimes wonder what my daughter and son will grow up to become. I consider their gifts and their personalities and assign career choices that I think would suit them, and they are no older than three! While I may be limiting their options, God has so much more in store for them, so much more than I can imagine and fathom. One day, I hope they will come to find their purpose, when they surrender their life to Jesus. Until then, I encourage them to try new things, to take leaps of faith and to grow up knowing they will always be loved, by me, by their Dad, and by Jesus.

Here are some ways to pray for purpose:

- Pray for strength in the season you are in.
- Ask God to reveal Himself to you, to show you what needs to be done and how He will use you.
- Pray that your children will grow up knowing God loves them and that He has a unique purpose for their lives.
- Ask God to encourage your heart and the hearts of your family so that you all may know that He has designed you wonderfully and perfect in His sight.

6

COMMUNITY

But Moses' hands grew weary, so they took a stone and put it under him, and he sat on it, while Aaron and Hur held up his hands, one on one side, and the other on the other side. So his hands were steady until the going down of the sun
– Exodus *17:12-13.*

Every time I read this verse, it makes me smile - what a great image of community and friendship. Moses was struggling, his arms were tired, they were going weak and aching at the elbows. Darn, I know that feeling, especially after the fourth load of clothing being hung out! Aaron and Hur, they could see Moses was struggling, the pain in his face, maybe even his arms were starting to shake so they sat by his side and helped him. They too lifted their arms to support Moses. Can you see this image in your mind? I can.

Motherhood can be so hard sometimes. You feel the ache, the sadness, tiredness, and sometimes I've found myself with no motivation to continue. But that's when we need to find our Aaron and Hur, someone to lift us up, to bring encouragement, maybe even to dig deep and cook our meals and clean our home.

Over the years this has been a longing desire in my heart. Having women in my life who I can turn to for advice, to shed tears, share my joys and to fellowship with, in my daily walk with God. It took me a long time to find these treasured women and there really aren't many of them. But that's ok. They're there, they know, they love big, cry with me, laugh with me, and are always available to chat any time of the day. Still, to this day, I am blown away by their grace towards me. The times they have delivered food to my door, sent me gifts just because, done my grocery shopping, held my daughter while I showered, came over during the night while I was going through my miscarriage and endless more. I thank God everyday for their blessing to me, and to my family.

I long for this closeness of community for my children. I want them to know who to turn to for advice and guidance when they may be too ashamed or embarrassed to tell their parents. My heart aches for them to have close friends to walk alongside them in this life. Good friends who will speak life into their hearts and tell them the truth when needed. Likewise, I want my children to see the hurt and the needs in others too. I want them to grow in wisdom, to be able to give good advice and lend a hand to those who are suffering.

At times, I also question whether I am a good enough friend. How do I share in the community? Perhaps, in the early years of motherhood we must surrender to the acceptance of help and support and then as time passes, we too can contribute to easing someone else's burden.

Our children will see those who come to the aid of their family. They will feel the love, the compassion, gentleness, and acceptance of those women (and sometimes men) who step up when needed. They'll know who their parents lean on when life gets tough, but they'll learn how to be that person when they watch their parents be that person too.

Here are some ways to pray for community:

- If you don't have a group of women to support you in motherhood, pray for God to bring them to you.
- Pray that your children will grow up with a loving and supportive community around them.
- Pray to have God's eyes and to be open to see the needs around you.
- Thank God for the blessings you're currently receiving from your community, whether that be family, friends, church, or workplace.

7
REST

*Come to me, all you who are weary
and burdened, and I will give you rest*
– MATTHEW 10:28.

Praying for rest is probably uncommon. Right now, life is busy; and you know what - it always will be. Every year there are new routines, class timetables, swimming lessons, and endless amounts of chores. Where is rest in the day-to-day? Or any rest for a mother, really? Furthermore, why is rest even important when there is so much to get done?

I'm sure many of you know the creation story - God creates the world in six days and then on the seventh day, he deems it "holy" and "rest[s] from the work he has done in creation" (Genesis 2:3). I remember hearing a sermon where the preacher said something along the lines of, "If God needs rest, so do we!" Mark 2:27 says, "The Sabbath, [a day of rest,] was made for man, not man for the Sabbath." So that preacher was right, to an extent, we do need rest. God has gifted us a day of rest, and it is up to us to receive the gift (a bit like peace) and use it.

I know there are seasons in my life where I feel like I just can't catch a break. One of my children is a big crier and has been from birth. The cry is exhausting, and my mind feels overstimulated by the noise. Some days I just feel like screaming and even crying alongside him. Where is rest in this?

Over the years, I have learnt that I need to create moments in my day, week, month, and year for rest. If I expect to just have rest, whenever, it won't happen. Rest, once accepted as a gift from God, does not actually have to take that much planning; it just needs to be used.

Consider this: what Genesis 2:3 calls rest is actually God quitting all normal activity. For Him, this was creating the world. What does quitting all normal activity look like for us? Does that mean, not cooking? Not cleaning? Not driving your kids to their extra-curricular activities? For me, it means a couple of those things, but also includes rest from work, rest from my phone, rest from the bombardment of voices that constantly speak to me throughout the day (Instagram and Facebook included). When we eliminate some of those things that rush us, hurry us, keep us busy and keep us distracted, we are provided with a blissful moment to hear God's voice. Rest provides a moment to be still.

Of course, mothers with little children may think this is impossible and an outrageous thing for me to consider, but rest is so important for you and likewise for your family. Think about your children and what they need rest from. Your husband too, what is something that he just needs to put a hold on or stop altogether, just for a day? I'm definitely not recommending that you just stop cooking altogether and get rid of your phone or pull your kids out of gymnastics. Instead, consider a day, just one day in your week that you all just stop your usual activity, your rushing, your planning and do something that fills you, restores you brings you closer to God and gives you strength to face the week ahead.

In our family, our weekly rest days are Sundays. I really don't like cooking (as you have probably gathered by now), so I attempt to ensure that our Sunday meals are planned on Saturday, so on Sundays I don't need to cook. I also attempt (although I really struggle with), putting my phone on silent or do not disturb on that day. By doing so I'm not getting distracted by every message that comes in and I don't feel tempted to even pick it up. For my husband, Sundays mean an afternoon nap or a walk to the park with the kids (which is great kid-free time for me). For our monthly rest days, we like to go camping as a family. We spend a weekend in our camper trailer, enjoying the outdoors, reading books, and going for walks. These are just a couple of examples of using the gift of rest and enjoying the blessing that comes from it. In these moments where life feels slower and calmer, we demonstrate that we actually can't do life without God. We forget our weariness and our burdens for an hour, a day or a weekend and lay them down at the feet of Jesus, allowing Him to sustain and provide for us for that period of time.

So, let's go back to the question, why do we pray for rest for our children? When I pray for rest, I ask God for moments in my children's day and week where they encounter God. I ask for moments of peace, stillness and quiet, where they learn to hear His voice.

Here are some ways to pray for rest:

- Ask God to show you what parts of your day you need rest from.

- Ask Him to give you the strength to just stop and be still for an hour, day, or weekend.
- Pray for rest and peace in your children, and that in those moments they learn to hear God's voice.
- Pray for God to reveal to you what fills you up after a long day, week, and month.

8
INTEGRITY

*Better is a poor man who walks
in his integrity than a rich man
who is crooked in his ways*
– Proverbs 28:6.

I remember the first time I heard of the word 'integrity'. I was probably about twelve years old and there was a member of our church congregation who stood up during free time to share a story about a student of his (he was a teacher) who did the right thing despite everything inside of him and around him tempting him to do wrong. This student was always known for getting into trouble, yet his teacher, in that moment, praised him for showing integrity. The young student didn't know what that meant, but once he did, his teacher recalled the young student's reaction. His heart was encouraged, he stood a little higher, and he was in shock that someone would regard him with such high esteem, considering that in most of his schooling years he had been given detention after detention and did not have a good reputation. His teacher, sharing these events, encouraged the congregation to speak words of life to young people, to encourage them to do what is right even when the whole world is doing wrong. He encouraged us to praise them, to support them and to notice when they choose to display integrity.

After hearing that story, my heart ached to be a woman of integrity. I wanted to be known for that very reason. Whenever I was faced with a decision, I would think back to this story. However, because I was never a *bad* student and I always tried to do what was pleasing to my parents and teachers, nobody ever noticed the days where my heart was pulled into temptation, and it took all of my strength to walk away. I craved someone to praise me, sometime to notice the hard moment of that situation. All I wanted was one word of encouragement to spur me on to keep doing the right thing.

We have so many of these kids in our lives, maybe even our own. Children who just seem to get into so much trouble *all the time*, and kids who just seem to go about their lives seemingly carefree, without worry and without disruptions. Regardless, each of these children need to hear our praise. Our praise when we see them do what is right, even when to us, that was seemingly obvious.

Integrity for a child is hard. No matter how many times I tell my children that right is right even when everyone is against it (thanks William Penn), everything is just so tempting, even unrolling that toilet paper roll for the hundredth time!

I read Proverbs 28:6 and I pose myself the question – is it really true? It is better to be poor and walk in integrity than rich but be crooked, perverse, unrighteous? Of course, it is. Life is not about materialistic wealth, it is about honouring God in our actions and words, and by being people who walk in ways which pleases Him alone. I want my children to learn to be good stewards of the wealth God has given them; but, being people of integrity, of honesty, goodness, and righteousness, is of much greater importance, because these are the attributes of their heart.

Here are some ways to pray for integrity:

- Pray that our children are protected from the evil in the world.
- Pray that God will open their eyes to the right thing to do and that He will give them the courage to do good, even when everything and everyone around them is tempting them to do wrong.
- Pray that they become people of integrity, people who are honourable, trustworthy, gracious and righteous in the eyes of God.
- Ask God to help you see the moments where your children are in conflict with doing good.
- Ask God to help you use words that speak life and encouragement into the hearts of your children and others around you.

9

IDENTITY

Know that the Lord is God. It is He who made us, and we are His; we are His people, the sheep of His pasture
— Psalm 100:3.

The word identity gets thrown around so much these days, it's hard to know what it even means. There's an element of fear when bringing it up. Do we offend? Are we being offended? I see identity as an element of belonging. Who do we belong to? Where do we fit in? Of course, identity can also mean so much more, but for my children, it is my desire for them to know their identity in Christ. There is nothing more important in this world than knowing who we are in front of God, and who we are through His eyes. We are His children, His beloved, and it is He who gives us value and worth.

This current world promotes many ideas of who we are and who we can become. It tells us to change this or buy that, to fix, pluck, pull, lift, speak, not speak. There is a push to discover who we are through a whole range of experiences and opportunities. Our western culture encourages our children to go out and find their true self in experiencing the world, and to listen to their hearts when unsure, but there is a fake freedom in inventing your own identity. As they search to find their gifts and talents, they find themselves slaves to the world and feeling burdened by this continual quest of self.

I believe we need to remind our children that they are a blessing from God, that they have His fingerprints imprinted on their hearts, that they are uniquely and intimately known by their Creator. Our children have a perfect place in our homes, in our families and our society. The Lord has already prepared a perfect plan for their lives and nothing about their arrival into this world is an accidental collision of cells. This is where their identity in Christ begins, in the knowing, understanding and believing that they are a child of God and nothing else in this world matters.

I often wonder what the development of a child to an adult would look like if they were constantly being encouraged to view themselves as a child of God. I hope to expect an adult (and growing child) to feel accepted and deeply loved. A person so secure in their place in this world and in the eyes of their family and ultimately God. What peace would surround their hearts and minds, as they grow up knowing that their identity, their place of belonging, is part of God's family. That God will make a way through the good and the bad times in their lives. There is no burden on their hearts as they try to find themselves, because they have already been found, identified, and loved for who they are. That's what the verse in Psalm is telling us; come to find your identity in Jesus, the one who "has made us", the one who call us "His", the one who provides "pastures" for us to enjoy.

Am I that confident in my identity with Christ? Do my kids see that?

Here are some ways to pray for identity:

- Pray that our children come to know the Lord intimately.
- Pray for their eyes and hearts to be opened to God's love for them and for them to never doubt this love.
- Ask God to make their paths clear to them, so that there is no doubt in the decisions they need to make.
- Ask God to use you to speak the truth into their hearts so that there is no doubt of the love you have for them, and God has for them.

10

TRUST

*Do not let your hearts be
troubled, trust in God*
− JOHN 14:1.

There are many times where my heart feels heavy. As a mother, there are seasons where I feel stretched to my limits and there doesn't seem to be enough hours in the day to get everything done. Often, things just don't go the way I plan them. Sometimes, I'm running late - the kids spill their cereal all over the kitchen floor, I've forgotten the clothes on the washing line and it has started to rain, or I've left my work laptop at home and have to turn the car around and pick it up. Kids get sick, we forget, and life just seems to get in the way. I feel the frustration rising inside of me and my reaction is to throw my hands up in the air and claim defeat. Where is God in this mess? Why do I feel so burdened by this life?

During the years of trying to conceive, there was a huge battle in my heart with trusting God. How could I trust that God is good when things were hard? How could I trust that He's in control when everything around me just seems like it's falling to pieces and when it looks like everything I have hoped for and dreamed of won't happen? How do I still trust God in these hard moments and continue with the commitment I made? How can I say yes to God despite what the circumstances around me are saying?

Just like in my season of waiting for a miracle, I try daily to remind myself to trust that God was working in the waiting. When our children are pushing us to our limits or we've been trying to toilet train for months, we need to trust that God is working in those moments. Trusting is hard at the best of times and even harder in the worst of times. But without it, we have nothing left in this world. We have no hope, no purpose; we have nothing to aspire to, nothing to look forward to. Nothing that will ease the burden of what we go through day by day.

Where we place our trust is just as important. If we place our trust in this world, we will always be disappointed. If we place our trust in our friends and family, we will be let down. If we place our trust in our work or careers, we'll always be dissatisfied. If we are always searching for the world to fill us, for people to define us, then we will always be discontent. We need to put our trust in Jesus. He is the one who will not change and has not changed throughout the ages, and we need to teach our children to put their trust in Him too. Maybe we need to slow down our days or take time to read with our kids on the couch. Maybe we need to go outside, get some fresh air, look up at the sky and take a deep breath. We choose who we trust. In those moments, choose Jesus.

This afternoon I was reminded of God's care for the birds in the sky, that they will not grow hungry because He feeds them (Matthew 6:25-33). My mind considered what it would be like for a bird, not having to worry about food, and knowing that it will always be in supply. There is trust, in some form, and a reliance on God to look after them. That verse in Matthew continues with, "Are you not of more value than they?" A direct question to me, one would say a rhetorical question – of course I am more valuable than a bird! Then why is it, that there are days that we feel that our spirit is troubled, that we don't feel like we are being cared for or looked after, or even valuable?

Our trust in God does not rely on feelings. Emotions are fleeting, they change and sway in the wind. One small incident can change our peaceful day into one that is filled with rage. God's word though, His power, and His deep love for us, is never changing. Dr Michael Kruger once said, "You can't let [your feelings] be the determining factor; you have to anchor into scriptural truth even if it's hard… That is the heartbeat of the Christian life: following God's word even if it doesn't make sense to us." We are not to let our emotions take over our hearts or cloud our minds. At times, our emotions can feed us lies about how much God doesn't want to hear from his children, when He so desperately does.

Our children will face hard days. We wish we could stop that from happening, but that's the reality of life. There will be days when they feel defeated, crushed, and purposeless. They might have troubled hearts as young children, teenagers, young adults, and even as they become adults themselves. However, as mothers, our job is to pray for their burdens and teach them how to leave them at the feet of Jesus. Because in those hard days, we might not be there, but we know Jesus is. He can be their peace and comfort.

Here are some ways to pray for trust:

- Pray for your child's heart, that it may find rest in Jesus.

- Pray for good Christian people to be there to support your children on the hard days.
- Pray that your child learns to trust the Lord with all their hearts.
- Ask God to help you teach them to trust Him.
- Ask God to help you trust Him, especially on the hard days.

11
LOVE

*And now these three remain:
faith, hope, and love. But the
greatest of these is love*
– 1 Corinthians 13:13.

*L*ove encompasses so much in life. Really, what is life without love? What excites me about praying for love for our children, is that love is in all things. I firstly want my kids to know the love of God, I want them to feel secure in the love we have for them as parents, I want them to be compassionate and kind people, to be loving towards others, I want them to find love in a spouse, and to remain in love with the Lord all the days of their lives. Isn't that what all Christian mothers want for their children?

My daughter is currently at the age where love is bribed. She'll constantly remind me that if I don't follow through with *her* desires, she won't be my best friend anymore. Much to her disappointment, as her mother, I will always love her, despite if I am considered her best friend or not. This got me thinking though, do we sometimes bargain our love with God. Do we attempt to dangle a carrot in His face claiming that our love is on the line if He doesn't approve of our own wishes, dreams, and ideas? As I've mentioned many times, God's love, much like mine with my children, is never ceasing, He will always love me despite what I say and what I do.

As a family, we have a vision and a mission to love people on purpose. What that means is we want to be faithful to God in showing compassion to others, to die to self, to seek the best in others, be a comforter, an encourager, and to make a point of being kind to the people God has created in this world. Love is an emotion, but it is also an action. We want our children to be loving people, not to dress up their personalities, but to shine Jesus everywhere they go. When we pray for love over our children, we pray for God to be hidden deep in their hearts, so that when they see people, they see them through His eyes. As that beautiful hymn by Hugh Mitchell says: "Thy loving kindness is better than life." May our children's love mirror the love Jesus has for all humankind, one that is far greater than life itself.

In the Bible's well known love chapter found in Corinthians 13, love is defined in many ways; as being patient, kind, not envious, not proud, self-seeking or rude, it doesn't anger easily or keep a record of being hurt. Love protects, trusts, hopes, and perseveres. What a list to aspire to!

If we take the time to reflect on what that looks like in our everyday life, I know that I have a lot of work to do. I definitely need to show more patience and kindness towards my family. There are also days where I forget that I am the caretaker of my husband's heart, and I end up sharing a list of all his faults to the people around me.

The point is though, our kids are watching us, they see the daily moments where we choose to die to our fleshly outburst and put on humility and grace. They see love when we are present in the moment or when we say a kind word and speak to them with grace in the middle of the night when we've been woken up for the fifth time. I know it is difficult, our hearts so desperately want to kick and scream, but we need to choose to love and show love. I'm sure there are endless ways you can do that for your own family and your own circumstances.

Here are some ways to pray for love:

- Ask God to help you love your husband and your children well.
- Ask God to help you show love towards them, especially on those hard days when it doesn't come naturally.
- Pray for your children's hearts, that they may grow to love God passionately and wholeheartedly.
- Pray for God's love to surround your family and your children, especially as they grow.
- Ask God to help your children shine his love to others around them, to love people with purpose.

12
VISION

Train up a child in the way he should go and when he is old, he will not depart from it
— Proverbs 22:6.

I can't help but sing the song "Be Thou My Vision" when I think of vision as a prayer word. I guess to some extent, the song speaks into what praying for vision is about. I've heard this hymn being described as a prayer to God that He is the first thing we seek after and the God we continually refocus our direction of our life to. This beautiful hymn is bracketed with "Be thou my vision, o Lord of my heart" and "Still be my vision, o ruler of all." It is reiterating our prayerful desire for God to be the one we pursue with our hearts, and the one we continue to trust throughout our lives.

When we pray for vision, we also pray for God to inspire the hearts of our children. It is similar to having a purpose, but with vision, there is a goal, something to aspire to. I love the way Jeremy Pryor describes a vision as "God's… calling on your kid's heart," The importance of having a vision, ties to having an identity. When our children know who they are in Christ, they desire to seek His will in their lives; it is then easier for our children to understand who, what, when and why they have been placed in this world, in this moment and generation.

The verse in Proverbs is merely a reminder to us as mothers of our job to train the hearts of our children. While they are young, while they are searching and seeking God's will. We should be encouraging our kids to look out for others, to find out their own skills and talents and to find their passion or something that stirs within their hearts and wants to make a change or stand for something. It's more than that too. The hymn reminds us that we should be placing God above all things in our lives, He is to be at the forefront of our minds. While our children are discovering God's vision for them, they continually seek His direction, His desires for their lives.

As mothers, we probably feel like this is a huge task. Perhaps something that feels way out of our depth. This whole training and moulding and shaping, how can we do this for one child, let alone multiple children!? May I remind you, and remind myself, we are only the vessels here. We are carrying the hearts of our children for such a short time, they are not ours, they are God's. In my prayer for vision, I continually ask God to show *me* the gifts and talents of my kids. I ask God to help *me* come to know them like He does. One day, when I have done my part in helping them, in seeking God on their behalf, their eyes will be opened to their next steps for Christ. I can't help but think how incredible it would be to finally see our children as adults living out their God given calling. Or better yet, to be there alongside them as they journey through some hard life moments and seeing them come out stronger, with a clearer vision.

Dear mothers, don't lose sight of the vision you cast onto your children. Ask God to help you see your kids, to really see them, with God's eyes. Then use that insight to encourage them to pursue their calling for their generation, so that they may never depart from the Lord and may be a blessing to others.

Here are some ways to pray for vision:

- Ask God to give you the eyes to see your children the way He sees them.
- Ask God to show you the strengths and weaknesses of your children, and where He has placed their unique gifts and talents.
- Pray that your children come to hear the calling on their hearts and to be faithful to that calling.
- Pray for obedience to step out in faith when the time is required.
- Ask God to help you train and equip your children for this generation.
- Pray for God to remind you, and your children as they grow, to always seek Him first above all things.

13

KNOWN

*You have searched me,
Lord, and you know me*
– PSALM *139:1.*

I wonder how many times we have said or done something to be known. I cringe just thinking back to the many times in my teenage years when I said things to up note myself or make myself sound knowledgeable and *cool*. I know we've all been there. I imagine you too are probably thinking of an exact moment right now.

As we get older though, the feeling of being known comes from wanting to be validated. I remember when we were going through infertility how much I held onto hate in my heart. I wanted to be seen. At times, I wanted this hatred to be noticed. I wanted my situation to be understood. I wanted to be known.

What I came to quickly realise is that I was, and always am, seen by God. During my heartbreak, He wanted me to seek refuge in Him, to pour out my bitter heart, know that I was validated in Him and rest in the knowledge that His plan is good and perfect for my life. There are times were I still feel like this, for various reasons. I'm sure there are times where your emotions and your fears or moments of heartbreak need a place of rest. We've probably moved away from wanting to be known to be popular, but now wanting to be known and seen in our pain, in our hurting and even sometimes in our moments of joy.

In our day-to-day life, there are moments as mothers where we find ourselves feeling unloved, unnoticed, and probably very disconnected. I've been feeling the pressure of it lately. The pull of needing to be everywhere for everyone, the need to please, the need to be present; yet in all of that, we push aside our discomfort, and we miss the moments of happiness. Sometimes it's as though we need to scream out if anyone can hear us, if anyone can see all the *things* we are doing for everyone else, and the *things* we are missing out on for ourselves. But that's just it, they are *things*. Pressures we put on ourselves and expectations that are probably all in our minds. Yet God sees us in this frantic rush throughout our lives, He's watching and He's waiting for us to come to Him for rest, for peace, and to come to Him to be seen. He is the one who knows us intimately and deeply and He is the one ready to sit and listen to our heart's desires, our worries, our fears and all the little things in between. He wants to reassure us, to be given the freedom to show how much He knows us and loves us.

As a teacher, I see how students act in my class when they want to show off their knowledge and skills. I see how their eyes light up when they know the answer to a difficult question, or when their faces frown as they grapple with ideas they can't put into words, I see their shoulders slump as they come into class first thing in the morning with very little sleep. In those moments, it is my voice that makes a difference. I praise, I encourage, I help give perspective and sometimes I'm silent, to make sure they have a safe place to share their burdens. I want my students to feel like they are known in my room. I want them to feel supported, validated, heard, and acknowledged.

I think of God in this way, I imagine Him listening intently to my grumblings, crouching down at my feet when I am weary. I imagine His smile when I've accomplished something, the joy in His eyes when He sees me smile through the hurt. In those moments, I know I am seen, I am validated, I am known, I am His.

Our kids will face times in their lives where they may feel something similar. Maybe they will want to fit in, to be invited, to be included. Maybe they had a proud moment at school that nobody else knows about, but it fueled them with joy for the day. Maybe they are too afraid to share their deepest thoughts or they're just not sleeping well, and mornings are hard. Whatever it might be, as mothers, we'll want to swoop right in and fix it. We'll want to act, say something sincere, or give a hug; but maybe that's not what our child needs or wants. Sometimes too, in the busyness of life, we miss these cues. We just don't see the hurt, the pain, or the joy on the face of our children. This is when God steps in. We ask Him to fill the void, to remind them that He is near; He sees, He knows, He provides comfort, and He is filled with joy when He sees our triumphs.

Psalm 139 is a powerful Psalm. As you read more than just the first verse, you'll soon see how known we are by God because we are formed by His hand. He discerns our thoughts, knows what words we'll say, is acquainted with where we are going, and knows our physical bodies better than anyone else. In the early years of motherhood where our bodies do not feel like our own, or our minds are clouded from lack of sleep, God is at work, watching over, paying attention to, and ensuring we are looked after. Inside of us, there is something that keeps us going.

When we and our children desire to be seen, to be validated and known, let us remember Luke 12:7, God knows the numbers of hairs on our heads, He knows more about us than anybody else.

Here are some ways to pray for your children to be known:

- Ask God to help you see your children the way He sees them, to give you wisdom in dealing with the seasons that come, so that you may be able to see when they struggle and to see their joys and know them well.
- Pray for God to remind your children that they are known and loved by Him.
- Ask God to remind you that you are seen by Him, in all the ordinary and mundane tasks of the day, all the highs and lows, you are His child.
- Pray for wisdom in the moments where our children need to be noticed.
- Ask that God provides the words and actions that will speak into the hearts of your children.

14

PATIENCE

*Therefore, as God's chosen people,
holy and dearly loved, clothe
yourselves with compassion, kindness,
humility, gentleness, and patience*
– COLOSSIANS 3:12.

We're all waiting for something, aren't we? I can hear all the questions I asked in my journey to motherhood: When will my body cooperate? When will I fall pregnant? When will I have a baby? And for other things in life too: When will I get a job? When will I have enough money to buy that home or go on that holiday? When will I be taken on that romantic dinner? When can I buy those new pairs of shoes? The list can go on and on. Honestly, I ask these questions and more each day.

I also know in my household, when I reply to my kids with "just wait", "give me a second" or "please be patient," these words are met with outburst, tears and sometimes fury. I can hear all the whining and crying as I type. Even as adults, we find it so hard to wait and be patient. In our waiting we are usually met with that famous proverb that "patience is a virtue."

There are countless verses in the Bible that talk about being patient. I don't know about you, but when I read these verses, I sometimes think that God wants me to be idle. I recently did a synonym search for patience, just out of curiosity, and a couple of the words really struck me: endurance, persistence, perseverance, forbearance. God doesn't want us to be stagnant in our waiting, He wants us to endure through the daily struggle, to be persistent in prayer, persevering through the delays, forbearing when the wait gets hard. God wants us to show endurance in the wait, without giving up hope.

Nine months of pregnancy can feel like torture. Our bodies ache, our minds are clouded and getting dressed seems like the most impossible task. We long for the day we get to hold our new baby in our arms, and that last week of pregnancy feels like an eternity. Everything inside of us desires for this wait to be over, even the grandparents are getting antsy. Yet, we're patient, aren't we? We have to be because the development of our child inside our womb takes time. We spend nine months arranging furniture, buying clothes, getting car seats ready and preparing for this little babe to be born. Although, we would love to, we don't sit in bed for nine months just waiting for the due date to come around.

Being patient in life is much the same - we need to keep up the fight, keep doing what we're doing, prepare for what is to come and sometimes keep reminding ourselves that our life is in God's hands. His timing is perfect, no matter how impatient we get.

Our little children don't understand the value in learning how to wait at a young age. Right now, the things that they are being patient with might seem trivial, but as they grow, these little things become big things. They start learning how to be patient with others, to be kind and gracious, to petition God in prayer, to wait for answers, to be led where God wants them to go, and so much more. I'm finding that this learning to be patient never really ends. Even now, I'm in a season of waiting and I'm reminding myself to do much the same.

Colossians 3:12 says that as children of God we should clothe ourselves with patience (among other things). We are to rest in the fact that we are "holy and dearly loved" - we are not forgotten, our answer will come, our time will come. If not now, then most definitely in heaven.

Here are some ways to pray for patience:

- Ask God to help you show patience to your children.
- Pray for the things you are waiting patiently for, and ask God to help you wait on Him.
- Ask that God gives your children a spirit of patience and that this may grow throughout their lives.
- Ask God to help your children (and yourself) be patient in the hard times and in those difficult seasons.

15
SELF-CONTROL

Every athlete exercises self-control in all things. They do it to receive a perishable wreath, but we are imperishable. So, I do not run aimlessly; I do not box as one beating the air. But I discipline my body and keep it under control
– 1 Corinthians 9:25-27.

It's probably an odd thing to pray for self-control for our children. I have learnt ever so quickly, my own need to grow in this area. While my child is throwing a tantrum, my husband is disagreeing with me, my sister is frustrating, and my friend tells me some honest truths. It's in those moments that I must choose to say 'no' to sin. I choose to not let the devil tempt my heart, my mind, my words, and my actions. Sometimes, self-control requires me to hold my tongue, sometimes it looks like me walking away, sometimes it's something totally different. But I know, in all those circumstances, how hard it is to turn away from my sinful nature and cave into the explosion of words and outbursts. I love the way Scott Hubbard describes how "God meets us in that dreadful moment and tells us how we can meet our sin at the door, hear its desperate pleas, and still say 'no'".

Motherhood has a way of showing us our flaws. I would say self-control is my biggest. I often reflect on how much God shapes us in every season. We are not perfect people, we are not perfect mothers, but we are children of God. It is through Him that we first have the realisation of our sin, then the strength to learn how to overcome it. Trust me, I know this is not easy. I cringe at the thought of the many times I have disciplined my children over self-control, yet I know that I so desperately need to work on it myself.

Praying for self-control for our children, or any flaw in our own character is hard, honestly, it feels a bit hypocritical. But my heart's desire is that my children don't pick up characteristics from me, instead they are beacons of the characteristics of their heavenly father. Training and discipline is not about us as parents, it's not to show off how good our parenting skills are, nor is it about dressing up the personalities of our children; it is all about Jesus. It is about having the character and personality of our loving God being reflected in our children's lives, from now as they are young, and as they continue to grow into adults. How wonderful it would be for our children to become adults and no longer have the desire to fall into the trap of losing self-control.

Losing self-control is letting our flesh overflow into our lives. As children of God, we need to learn how to crucify the flesh so that we are serving God fully. The verse in 1 Corinthians metaphorically compares an athlete training their body for a materialistic prize, and a Christian training their body to reflect Christ to non-believers, a prize that has eternal impact. We are here to do just that, be imitators of Christ and reflect Him to all people, and this is done in the way we show self-control. Let us crucify our old selves, put to death our flesh, and walk, speak, act, eat and drink in ways that show we are new creations in Jesus. My desire, and I'm sure it also yours too, is to be a mother who firstly reflects Jesus to her children and secondly, brings these little hearts to Him.

Perhaps during your days, weeks, months, or years into motherhood, God has revealed characteristics in you that don't reflect His nature. Perhaps, you see them begin to reflect in the personalities of your own children. It may be self-control, it may be something else; however, we have an opportunity now to bring these before God, to stop the flesh from taking over and pray for them specifically.

Here are some ways to pray for self-control:

- Ask God to reveal to you the characteristics in you and your children that don't reflect Him and His nature.
- Ask God to help you gain self-control in those hard, frustrating, and tedious moments, especially when dealing with your children and your spouse.
- Pray for God to help your children with their own battles against their fleshly desires.
- Pray for wisdom in disciplining and training your children to be imitators of Christ, especially in the way that they control their words and actions.

16
TEACHABLE

*Teach me your way, Lord, that
I may rely on your faithfulness;
give me an undivided heart,
that I may fear your name
– Psalm 86:11.*

We want our children to be able to persist through challenges, to face things head-on. We want them to have soft hearts, ready to learn and grow in all areas of their lives. When they are young, this looks like growing in character, as they get older, this may be academically, as adults it may be in the way they depend on God throughout all seasons of life.

I remember having a student in my class who was a brilliant writer. Her poems moved me to tears, and her analysis of texts were deep and thoughtful. However, when it came to exam time, she couldn't perform. Upon reflection, she would tell me how she didn't feel good enough or didn't want to write something down in case it was wrong. There was a fear of letting herself down and mostly, a fear of failure. After many discussions, she finally revealed to me that she also dreaded feedback. She didn't want to know how she could improve, because the task just seemed too big to deal with and being teachable just wasn't her thing (those were her exact words).

We need to remember that growth is in the process. I have mentioned before how God cares more about the journey than the destination. He cares more about your development in character, the fine tuning of your heart, than the end result. If that were not so, he would immediately take us up to heaven as soon as we proclaimed to give Him our life. He wouldn't care about your time here on earth, and how you have come to know and to love him through the journey of life.

As you reflect on your own life, I'm sure that there are seasons where you see yourself being stretched and challenged. Seasons where you are impressed that you made it through. I've heard so many times in my hard moments that God will never give us more than we can handle. We try to take comfort in those words because they come with good intentions, but 1 Corinthians 10:13 tells us that God may give us more than we can handle in our own strength. But *with* Him, we can endure.

When we face a season of growth, we may find ourselves stretched beyond our limits. The early days of motherhood can at times feel like that with the crying babies, the constant feeding, the sleepless nights, and if you have more than one child, the demands of the rest of the family. We may be burdened and lack peace; we may forget that we should have the confidence of God's will in our lives. We may feel hard pressed, *but* we are being refined.

Let us surrender ourselves to God in these moments of growth. Let's attempt to have a teachable spirit. So, just like Psalm 86:11 says, that we rely on the faithfulness of God and not our own abilities. Let us teach our children to do the same; to ask God for His direction, for His opinion of them, so that they may grow in His ways and not the ways of the world.

Here are some ways to pray for a teachable spirit:

- Pray that God softens your heart, and the hearts of your children during tough seasons, so that you may grow into a deeper relationship with the Lord.
- Ask God to give you a teachable spirit, to come to know your weaknesses and to have the courage to leave our fleshly desires.
- Ask for strength and courage in your season of growth and in your child's season of growth.

17
MOMENTS

> *I will remember the deeds of the Lord*
> – P<small>SALM</small> 77:11.

Have you ever had a moment in your life where you have heard God speak to you so clearly, you couldn't deny it? Have you ever felt God lead you to a place you never would have gone? Or lead you to speak when you wanted to remain silent? While our faith doesn't depend on feelings or actions, we know that in those moments, the Holy Spirit has spoken to us directly, this is what I like to call a 'God moment'.

God moments are those inexplainable and undeniable times in our lives that our hearts and minds are so tuned in with Christ that we hear Him speak and we see Him work in and around us. It is those little moments (and sometimes big moments) that our faith is tested and refined. We step out knowing that God is in control, and He is leading us through. God uses the gifts and talents that He has bestowed on us to use us for a particular time. He calls us to encounter Him, rely on Him and be changed by Him.

I desire for my children to have such a deep relationship with Jesus that they too have these God moments. I want them to look back on their lives and see where God has used them, spoken to them, changed them and sustained them. There are important lessons to be learnt in those times. Things that they can one day share with their own children, a legacy that can be left for future generations. What a precious thing for God to meet us where we are at, to encounter Him and to know that He is fully present in our lives.

As a mother, it can be so easy to fixate my daily life around dishes, cleaning, cooking, outings, washing, and of course, my paid job as a teacher. The day quickly passes before I realise that I haven't sat fully present at the feet of Jesus, my busyness has prevented me from sustaining my relationship with my Lord. My kids will see this. They will notice how I go about life doing *it all* but not doing the most important thing *of all*. We need to seek out moments to be with Jesus. We need to prioritise this. I know how difficult it is; I am literally speaking to myself here. But, if I want my children to seek God, if I want them to see that my most important relationship is with Him, then I need to show that in my life.

I'm sure your children mimic so many of your actions and words; I know mine do. Oftentimes, my husband and I will look at each other in amazement at the words and phrases that come out of our daughter's mouth and hope that the words we said in frustration and annoyance aren't repeated too! That leads us to question though, what is in our daily and weekly rhythm that our children will mimic? How do we share our perspective on daily life that brings Jesus at the centre of it all? Will they learn to have moments of quiet reflection? Will they learn to listen to His voice?

The ending of Psalm 77 was one that really struck me at the start of this year. As I was reading verses ten through to fifteen, I recalled the moments throughout the last few years that God has blessed me, God has been with me, and He has sustained me. Verse 11 says, "I will remember the deeds of the Lord," and I will remember the things He has done. God has provided and He has taken care of my family and me. I truly see the moments I have encountered Jesus. I have seen Him at work and my faith has been made new because of it. Let us ask God for these moments for our children, so that they may one day look back and see the glorious works of our Lord.

Here are some ways to pray for moments:

- Ask God to bring about moments in the lives of our children that will help refine their faith.
- Ask God to help you see the moments of everyday life through His eyes so that our children see how we can glorify Him.
- Pray that God reminds you of those moments where He has sustained you and provided for you.

18

HOPE

> *But those who hope in the Lord*
> *will renew their strength*
> – Isaiah 40:31.

Motherhood can be tough at times. Sometimes we doubt if what we are doing is enough, sometimes we wonder if this season will ever get easier, at times we question if we have the strength to keep going. Sometimes our tears fall, and yet every day we make the choice to choose love and to press on with hope.

I've been in contact with a few adoptive mothers over the years. Their children have come to them with broken hearts and spirits, and these mothers are desperately trying to bring hope into the life of their child. Mothers who have felt misunderstood, especially those who have journeyed through infertility, attempt to bring hope and comfort to those who unfortunately know exactly what that feels like. There are some mothers who feel forgotten and abandoned over the years and they hold onto the hope that the future will be better. Motherhood, in its many forms, is a beautiful and redeeming thing, occasionally, given the circumstances, some of that redemption comes wrapped up in so much brokenness, pain and loss, but there is always hope.

I love the quote by John Green that says: "The nature of impending [motherhood] is that you are doing something that you're unqualified to do, and then you become qualified while doing it." God takes such risk to entrust us with the hearts and lives of our children. He loves us so much that He trusts us to be parents. Our strength will be renewed when we put our everyday bits into the hands of Jesus. We need to rest in Him, take delight in Him, and spend time with Him. We have hope in Jesus. Yes, this season might be a struggle, being a mother doesn't look as wonderful as you had imagined it. Your child might be testing you and you might be in a period of confusion and hurt, but let's aim to raise our children with hope and to know that they are children of God.

This book results from my own moments of seeking hope. Moments I desired to be close to God and times where I felt heavy laden and burdened by the what ifs and just waits. There are still days that I am just hanging to see the light at the end of the tunnel.

Third Day's song, *Cry Out to Jesus*, is a great encouragement to me when I am in those moments:

> ...'And to all of the people with burdens
> and pains
> Keeping you back from your life
> You believe that there's nothing and there
> is no one
> Who can make it right'
>
> There is hope for the helpless
> Rest for the weary

And love for the broken heart
And there is grace and forgiveness
Mercy and healing
He'll meet you wherever you are
Cry out to Jesus…

…When you're lonely
And it feels like the whole world is falling on you
You just reach out, you just cry out to Jesus…'

Our world is losing hope at a rapid rate, yet we know that Jesus is that answer to all the searching and confusion. Where does our hope come from? When it all just feels too much, who do we turn to? Let's do what this song suggests and cry out to Jesus. He so desires that we do.

Here are some ways to pray for hope:

- Pray for God to give you hope during the tough days.
- Ask God to help you see past the moment you are in, to look ahead and to have your eyes fixed on Him.
- As we are trusted with the hearts of our children, ask God to help you bring hope into their lives.
- Pray for God to use you in your community to be a beacon of hope and life to others around you.

19

GODLY PERSPECTIVE

Take your everyday, ordinary life—your sleeping, eating, going-to-work, and walking-around life—and place it before God as an offering. Embracing what God does for you is the best thing you can do for him. Don't become so well-adjusted to your culture that you fit into it without even thinking. Instead, fix your attention on God. You'll be changed from the inside out. Readily recognize what he wants from you, and quickly respond to it. Unlike the culture around you, always dragging you down to its level of immaturity, God brings the best out of you, develops well-formed maturity in you
– ROMANS 12:1-2.

Courtney Reissig talks about how "we are living in a time when being ordinary is the worst thing that can happen to a person." If you ask any person on earth, especially our teenagers, there is an innate desire to be something and do something with their lives. Our society pushes this agenda too.

We are defined by our jobs, our titles, what cars we drive, what clothes we wear and what we do during our holidays. Ordinary just doesn't cut it in this world. Ordinary is boring. Ordinary is lifeless. Or so it seems.

I love the message version of Romans 12:1-2 because it really highlights how the ordinary life – the "sleeping, eating, going-to-work, and walking-around life" is not at all ordinary to God. What seems to us as unexciting and useless, and maybe just practical, God sees as a place of service to Him. God delights in these everyday moments; He sees them as valuable to furthering His kingdom. When we change our perspective on these humble, "everyday, ordinary" tasks, we come to notice that they are not meaningless.

It was explained to me once how Moses' staff was just a piece of wood, yet under God's authority, this staff could part waters. Moses had to loosen his grip, he had to turn this staff over to God for these miracles to take place. We too, need to loosen the tight grip we have on our lives, and the worldly perspectives that bombard our minds about what is worthy is this world. We need to turn every small detail and authority of our lives over to God so that we can be useable to Him. When we do so, our everyday becomes meaningful instead of meaningless, because our perspective has changed. It becomes all about Him, instead of all about me and my gain.

How wonderful it would be if our children saw that their everyday life could be worship to God. I wonder how their hearts would change when they had this perspective that God still delights in them, even in the ordinary. Even when they wake up late for school, when they are sitting in class, when they are the last ones to get picked for the team, when they feel unloved;

God cares so deeply about them because He created them. The day they are living is important to God, the day they have before them is important to Him. *Every*thing, *every* time, *every* day.

The second part of this verse talks about how we shouldn't be "dragged down" by the culture around us. Our culture is filled with easy fixes, daily inspirations and what seems to be bigger and better adjustments in life. The truth is, we will never keep up, there is always more to have, more to own and more to behold. We will never be satisfied. Our culture is 'immature', but it is God who brings out the best in people. A well-formed version of you is made when we rely on God, rest in His promises, and seek to worship Him in all that we have, big or small.

Let's aim to have this perspective for ourselves and our families. May our children grow knowing that they are truly loved by God and that their lives matter to Him. Our hope is that they have a godly perspective throughout their life and that this isn't clouded by what the world says to them.

Here are some ways to pray for a godly perspective:

- Ask God to help you see how your everyday life and ordinary tasks can be used as worship to Him.
- Ask God to actively show your children how God cares about the smallest details of our lives, so that they grow to have that same perspective.
- Pray for your children, that their perspective is not tainted by the world, instead is fixed on God and His truths found in the Bible.

He who has ears to hear, let him hear
– MATTHEW 11:15.

During my last week of work before starting my maternity leave, I was inundated with so many kind words and gifts for the safe arrival of our baby. In my staff prayer group, I received cards with bits of advice, which each member in the group read to me. A lady who was placed randomly in this group with me, told me to continually pray for the salvation of my child. While at the time I thought that was probably a given, I've come to realise that I may be the only person in the world, apart from my husband of course, that would be praying over my child, especially in the early years. We prayed diligently to bring our children into this world, and we should continue to do so now that they are here, and likewise with any other added children we are blessed with.

It is also my own salvation I need to pray for. At times all I can pray about is for God to strengthen my own faith in Him. I need salvation just as much as my daughter, husband, family, and friends. Sometimes this word of prayer is just for me. A reminder of what I have promised to the Lord of the world – my heart. Praying for my salvation is paramount, it is powerful in those days when I need to remember who my God is, what He can do and how I have pledged to follow Him, to obey Him and rest in Him all the days of my life. It's not about questioning whether I am saved, but more about reminding myself that I am, despite how I look or feel in the trenches of motherhood.

When we decide to pray for salvation, what do we really mean? I believe, what we're really asking God is that our hearts, our ears, our minds, and our eyes are attuned to Him so that we can know, love and worship God with everything we are and everything we have. This is what the verse in Matthew 11:15 reminds me to do.

Salvation also means to be rescued or saved. I want my family and my child to be protected from sin, death, hurt, pain, fear, frustrations, and the things that this world offers. But I can't save them, I have no authority or power to do so. God is the only one who can save them from this. We want our children to hear God, to see Him, taste Him, to love Him with all their hearts so that they can then trust in His power to protect them and help them in this world. I want the assurance of eternity stamped on their hearts. One day my children will be old enough to make decisions for themselves, including the decision to follow Christ. I will have no control over their choice, but I do have the choice to pray for them from a very young age for their hearts and their mind to soften towards God's love, so that when that decision needs to be made, they will already know the God who is calling them.

As our children grow from infancy, into their early years, into teenage years, young adults, and adults; we want them to have Jesus as the foundation of their personal lives. We know that this is a life-long endeavour, which sometimes proves to be difficult and challenging. We know that, as mothers, we are not always the best examples of living Christian lives, but we also know that a life with God is better than anything else this world can offer. We know that with diligence, humility, deliberate reflection and faithfulness, our God makes all things new and all things perfect. He provides all joy, peace, purpose, rest, identity, love, vision, patience, self-control, growth, moments, trust, hope, and perspective.

So how could I not include salvation in a book about praying for our children? At the centre of this book and all these words of prayer, is the deepest desire as mothers to see our children come to know and love God with all of their hearts. We know that when this happens, nothing else in this world matters. Sometimes you'll need to pray for your salvation and many times it'll be a prayer of hope for your children. Maybe if this prayer comes naturally to you, pray for the children in your circle of friends too – your nieces, nephews, neighbourhood children, children in your church or mother's group. You may be the only one praying for them.

Here are some ways to pray for salvation:

- Pray that God reminds you of the promise you made to commit your life to Him.
- Ask God to flag moments in your day as reminders of who He is, what He has done for you and why you decided to follow Him.
- Pray for the hearts of your children to soften towards the Lord.
- Ask God to give your children eyes to see, ears to heart and hearts to love Jesus.

- Pray that your children will come to know and love the Lord all the days of their life.

FINAL THOUGHTS

Our lives are constantly busy, and sitting to pray may be the very last thing you want to do; I know that feeling well. But let me encourage you, dear mothers, that our children, our families, and our husbands need our prayers. We learn to pray by praying, we learn to sit at the feet of Jesus by being still. Prayer is powerful. In every season, at any time, we need to pray. We pray because God hears; He knows, He cares, He loves, He heals, He restores, He'll bring hope when there doesn't seem like there is a way out. Charles Spurgeon writes that "Short prayers are long enough" and that's what I hope you've come to see in this book. He continues by saying, "There were only three words in Peter's petition, but they were sufficient for his purpose. Not length, but strength, is desirable… if our prayers had more of the wing and less of the tail feathers of pride, they would be all the better." Let us set aside our pride, our to-do lists, those things that seem drastically important, and simply bring before God our words.

If prayer comes easy to you, I urge you to use these words as inspiration to pray for your sisters in Christ, their children, and their families. What a different world we can live in when we start praying for the women in our lives instead of comparing and talking about each other. As Lauren DeMoss Benson writes, "While women all over the world are fighting for "a seat at the table", let us be the women found at Jesus' feet."

My hope is that you disregard all that is written in human weakness. While I hope to have encouraged, supported, and inspired you, remember to seek Jesus first. My words are meaningless without Him, and they will be meaningless to you if your focus is elsewhere in life. I have shared my heart and I have challenged myself while writing this book, but my goal is that as mothers we see our value and purpose in the way that we raise the next generation of children who are passionately in love with Jesus and share His love to the world.

Finally, I urge you, don't give up praying, and be persistent with your prayers. You may not see the fruit of your words immediately, but you are growing your intimate relationship with your maker. Luke 18:1 says, "Jesus told His disciples… that they should always pray and not give up." Make that your mission in life.

ACKNOWLEDGEMENTS

Firstly, to the king of my heart, the one who made it all and knows me best. May all glory be given to You.

My proof-reader, helpmate, best friend, joker, prayer warrior, husband. I am so glad that I get to spend this life with you. Thank you for always pushing me to seek God's best, to never doubt what He has placed on my heart, and for never saying I was crazy or out of my depth, even if you were thinking it. You've been my biggest support from the very beginning, this book wouldn't be here without your encouragement.

My children, I see God's faithfulness in you. What a joy it is to be your Mum.

Dad and Mum, thank you for your constant prayers throughout my life. You have taught me what it means to be faithful, honest, and hardworking. I couldn't be more thankful for the life you sacrificed for us growing up, and for the constant support you show our family now.

My favourite in-laws, you have loved me like your own daughter. I am forever grateful for the joy and love you bring to our family. Thank you for always being fervent in your prayers for us.

My siblings, who always keep me accountable, honest, and encourage my crazy endeavours.

Josephine, my cheerleader, and biggest support. You were the first person I talked to about this book, while it was still a dream. Thank you for your encouragement, your truth, and your grace. You are a huge blessing to me, and I admire your own dedication to pray for your children.

My 'gal pals' - Jessica, Priscilla, Namrata and Josephine, you ladies are a prayer fulfilled. You've all been there from the beginning and have spoken so much wisdom into my life as a mother and daughter of Christ. Thanks for providing me a space to laugh, cry and ask random questions.

My colleagues who have become some of my closest friends, I won't and can't name you all, but you know who you are. You have all been there for me in different ways throughout the years. You have watched me struggle with prayer, struggle with hope and have helped walk me through the pain and confusion. Some of you are not mothers, but I have learnt so much from your guidance, love, and heart towards people. You are all true examples of strong Christian women.

Ark House and the publishing team, thank you for trusting me with this project and for giving me the opportunity to share this message.

Printed by BoD™in Norderstedt, Germany